The Aviation Notebook Series

BOEING 747

Stewart Wilson

Airlife
England

The first and the latest - so far. The 747 prototype (top) is a very different aircraft to the 747-400 of two decades later despite their outward appearances. Following generation 747s will represent an equally great leap in technology and efficiency.

Contents

Copyright © 2000 Stewart Wilson and Wilson Media Pty Ltd
First published in the UK in 2000
by Airlife Publishing Ltd

First published in Australia by Wilson Media Pty Ltd

British Library Cataloguing-in-Publication Data
A catalogue record for this book is available from the British Library

ISBN 1 84037 217 6

Production and design: Gayla Wilson and Wendy Wilson,
Special thanks to Australian Aviation. Colour profiles by Juanita Franzi.

Printed in Australia

Airlife Publishing Ltd
101 Longden Road, Shrewsbury, SY3 9EB, England
E-mail: airlife@airlifebooks.com
Website: www.airlifebooks.com

Queen Of The Skies

Sometimes, things don't go exactly according to plan, even if they are great events in the history of aviation. One of these occurred on 21 January 1970, the date for which the inaugural Pan American Boeing 747 service between New York and London was supposed to take place.

On that day, the scheduled evening departure from New York had to be postponed to early the next morning due to a series of problems which necessitated a change of aircraft and slightly subdued the grand occasion. And grand it was, with the world's largest and newest airliner departing on its maiden voyage after due ceremony in front of a large contingent of airline, industry and civic VIPs had taken place. It was history in the making but would have to wait just a little longer.

After the ceremonial duties had been completed, 336 happy and excited passengers boarded Pan American 747-121 N733PA *Clipper Young America* (the sixth aircraft off the line) in time for the scheduled 7.00pm departure from John F Kennedy Airport. But a door wouldn't close properly and then there was a delay loading cargo. Finally, the 747 began taxiing 25 minutes late, but when lining up for takeoff an engine overheating warning forced Captain Bob Weeks to bring the aircraft back to the terminal.

The passengers disembarked, but those planning the event had left nothing to chance and had another 747 standing by. The passengers eventually boarded N736PA *Clipper Victor*, this 747 hastily (and temporarily) rechristened *Clipper Young America* for the by now well delayed inaugural flight. N736PA finally got airborne from JFK at 1.52am on 22 January, arriving at London Heathrow 6hr 13min later.

The Boeing 747's commercial career was underway, albeit nearly seven hours late!

Air Transport Revolution

When discussing the history of air transport, it is impossible to understate the importance of the Boeing 747 as it truly revolutionised the industry just as the Douglas DC-3 and the early jet liners (notably Boeing's own 707) had done in years past.

As the world's first widebody, very high capacity jet airliner, the 747 introduced a new set of rules for the long haul carrier and passenger. The secret lay in that high capacity - over 400 passengers - because it reduced seat-mile operating costs to a point where economy class air fares could be cut to a level which made air travel affordable for nearly everyone.

This opened up a huge new potential market which in turn resulted in substantial increases in tourism to all points of the world and a consistent

The words 'dawn of a new era' are often overused, but when the first 747 flew on 9 February 1969 it really was. The commercial air transport industry was about to be revolutionised.

growth in travelling numbers over the more than three decades the 747 has been in service. With the advent of other widebody jets and the development of ever more efficient narrowbodies, it can't be said that the 747 was solely responsible for the revolution, but it was the pioneer, the aircraft which first made mass air travel possible.

While the sheer size and carrying capacity of the 747 permitted the operating economics which resulted in lower fares, the airframe was only half of the equation. It needed engines powerful enough to lift the world's heaviest airliner, but which would also offer improved specific fuel consumption, lower exhaust emissions and less noise.

Enter the 'big fan' high bypass ratio turbofans developed by Pratt & Whitney (JT9D), General Electric (CF6) and Rolls-Royce (RB211), all of which have found their way onto the 747 over the years. The JT9D as offered on the early 747s provided up to 25 per cent lower fuel consumption (on a seat-mile basis) than the JT3D first generation turbofans which powered the later 707s. Since then, the high bypass fans have been further developed to produce considerably more power while at the same time offering even better fuel consumption, noise and emissions characteristics.

The carriage of passengers is not the only area where the 747 has made a major contribution to the global economy. Air freight has also witnessed a 747 revolution, even in the passenger carrying versions which have an underfloor hold volume more than two-thirds that of the whole fuselage of a dedicated 707 freighter. This provided airlines with a substantial second source of revenue from the growing air freight market.

Then there's the Combi and dedicated freighter versions of the 747 which were introduced at an early stage of its career. The 747-400 freighter is capable of carrying a 273,350lb (124 tonnes) payload over a range of more than 4,000nm (7,400km), this level of capability offering those who want to send even very large items of freight the option of doing so by air in a fraction of the time taken by sea. The cost of air freight is still greater than sea

As it had done a decade earlier with the 707, Pan American was the airline which took the plunge and first ordered the 747. The American flag carrier contracted for 25 in April 1966, simultaneously launching the JT9D engine.

freight but as it has done with passenger travel, the 747 has made a substantial contribution to reducing that cost.

Military Origins

What finally emerged as the Boeing 747 airliner began life in mid 1962 as a series of design studies intended to meet the forthcoming US Air Force CX-HLS (Cargo Experimental Heavy Logistics System) requirement for a very large military transport aircraft capable of carrying a 125,000lb (56,700kg) payload over a range of 6,950nm (12,870km) or twice that load over a shorter distance. At the same time, the aircraft had to be capable of operating from the same runway lengths (and unprepared surfaces) as the smaller Lockheed C-141 Starlifter.

Several designs were investigated around the classic military transport configuration of high wings and rear loading ramp. The as yet unspecified four engines were mounted in underwing pods. Boeing, Douglas and Lockheed were invited to formally present proposals to meet the CX-HLS (later C-5A) requirement, Boeing committing more than 500 engineers to the task which culminated in the submission of a 4,272 page document in September 1964.

Further work followed and it was to Boeing's considerable disappointment that Lockheed was awarded the contract to build 63 C-5A Galaxy transports (plus options on a further 57) in September 1965. The first C-5A flew in June 1968 as the world's largest aircraft.

The Galaxy would be powered by four General Electric TF39 high bypass turbofans each of 41,000lb (182.3kN) thrust, this subsequently be developed into the civil CF6. Pratt & Whitney had invested six years developing its similarly rated JT9D turbofan for the C-5A contract and had also lost out. Both Pratt & Whitney and Boeing now turned to the commercial possibilities.

Towards 747

Even while the CX-HLS project was in its relatively early stages, Boeing had begun thinking about the possibilities of a very large airliner using some of the ideas and technologies which had been developed for the military transport. In 1963, the company's market research department had predicted the need for an airliner with twice the 707's passenger capacity for service in the 1970s.

Formal preliminary design work began in August 1965 and by the end of the year three different sized designs were under consideration under the designations 747-3, 747-4 and 747-5. All were mid wing designs (the high wing needed to accommodate a rear loading ramp in the military transport was unnecessary) with double bubble fuselages containing two passenger decks. Each deck had an internal width of 15ft 0in (4.57m), sufficient for seven abreast seating in a 2-3-2 configuration with two aisles.

Side-by-side bubbles were also briefly examined as were two decks inside a 'single bubble' fuselage and more than 14,000 wing tunnel hours were devoted to studying the aerodynamic properties of the various configurations.

The 747-3/4/5 studies were all smaller than the CX-HLS design with maximum takeoff weights ranging from 532,000lb (241,315kg) to 599,400lb (271,888kg) and passenger capacities from 311 to 433. Design cruise speed was Mach 0.90, range around 5,000nm (9,260km) with full passenger load and four engines in the 40,000lb (177.9kN) thrust class were envisaged. No decision as to the type of engine had been made by the end of 1965.

Airline reaction to the 'double decker' layout of the early proposals was generally negative, this forcing Boeing to look at single deck alternatives. Several variations were studied, culminating in the now familiar single deck and low wing configuration with a raised 'hump' for the flight deck and small passenger area behind it, initially intended as a first class lounge. The main cabin was able to extend right to the nose of the aircraft and the two levels were connected by a spiral staircase.

The final dimensions of the fuselage - especially those pertaining to width - were in reality dictated by as much by the decision to exploit the 747's freight carrying potential as anything else with the final main cabin internal width of 20ft 1^1/$_2$in (6.13m) sufficient to accommodate two 8ft x 8ft (2.44 x 2.44m) containers side by side. The cabin width allowed comfortable nine abreast economy class seating but 10 abreast (3-4-3) was also available and adopted by many carriers. It was therefore possible to carry up to 500 passengers but Boeing's early suggested configuration was for 368 passengers - 55 first class and 313 economy.

Including the flight deck level, the 747 as it finally emerged was really a triple deck aircraft if the two capacious underfloor luggage holds are taken into account, these providing 5,190cu ft (146.9m^3) of space for freight, mail or luggage. When details of the 747 first began to publically emerge, much was made of its 187ft 0in (57.0m) long cabin being about 50 per cent greater than the length of the Wright brothers' first flight. The sheer overall size of the aircraft attracted much attention with the popular press and public quickly applying the nickname 'Jumbo Jet' to the world's largest airliner.

Refining The Concept

Boeing began actively marketing the 747 in early 1966, at that stage against planned competition from the Lockheed L-500 (a commercial version of the C-5A) and Douglas, which was developing a twin deck, mid wing design similar to Boeing's earliest proposals under the name DC-10. That

A model with models! Some of the 747 concepts which were explored from 1965 including double decker and side-by-side 'double bubble' designs. The model at the front centre is the final configuration.

designation was subsequently applied to the smaller widebody trijet which first flew in August 1970, while Lockheed adopted a similar approach with the L.1011 TriStar (first flight November 1970).

Both Lockheed and Douglas were of the opinion that the market was not ready for an airliner of the size and capacity Boeing was offering but the latter stuck to its guns and in early March 1966 gave tentative approval for the project to go ahead, subject to various items of review.

At that stage the 747 was very similar to the aircraft that would finally emerge with a 183ft 10in (56.03m) wing span, wing sweep of 40 degrees, maximum weight of 625,000lb (283,500kg) and 16 wheel main undercarriage (to meet weight distribution requirements so that existing runways, taxiways and airport aprons could be used) comprising a quartet of four wheel bogies line abreast under the fuselage and wing centre section. The final 747 configuration was slightly modified with a wing span of 195ft 8in (59.64m), sweep of 37.5 degrees, proposed maximum weight of 680,000lb (308,448kg) and a revised main undercarriage layout in which the bogies were 'staggered' with the underwing units slightly behind those under the fuselage.

By this stage Pratt & Whitney (JT9D), General Electric (TF39/CF6) and Rolls-Royce (RB.178 and later RB.211) were all vying to have their engine on the 747. Both the latter pair were still projects at the time but the JT9D would begin flight trials under the wing of B-52 Stratofortress bomber in June 1968. The RB.211 first flew on a Vickers VC10 in March 1970.

Not for the first time, Boeing said it was 'betting the company' on the 747 with the aircraft's total development costs (including a new production facility, tooling up, materials, research and development etc) reckoned by some at around $US1 billion in 1960s terms - an enormous investment. A price per aircraft of around $US18.5m was quoted to the many airlines which had held discussions with Boeing. Apart from the basic passenger version, the aircraft was also offered in 747C mixed passenger/freight and 747F pure freighter versions, the latter with an upwards hinged nose forward of the flight deck to allow straight in loading.

The first 747 (appropriately registered N7470) was rolled out from Boeing's Everett facility on 30 September 1968 in front of a large crowd of dignitaries, airline executives, Boeing staff and guests. Few would have seen so big an aircraft.

The first 747 on an early test flight. The certification programme involved five aircraft and 1,013 flights. It was completed in December 1969, a remarkably short time considering the new ground being broken.

By March 1966 Boeing was projecting a first flight in the final quarter of 1968 with initial deliveries scheduled for a year later.

First Orders

As it had done a decade earlier with the 707 and Douglas DC-8, Pan American was the airline which took the plunge and placed the first order for the 747. On 13 April 1966 it contracted for 25 aircraft (including two freighters) worth $US525m, the largest single order in commercial aviation history to that point. Pan Am selected the JT9D to power its 747s, also launching that engine.

Even this was not sufficient for Boeing to finally commit itself to building the 747. That had to wait until 25 July 1966 after Japan Air Lines and Luftwaffe had each ordered three examples of the new airliner. After that, it became very much a case of other major international airlines having to order the 747 or be left behind, much as had happened in the late 1950s when the 707 and DC-8 became available, resulting in something of an ordering frenzy.

By the end of 1966 Air France (4), Alitalia (4), American Airlines (10), BOAC (6), Northwest (10), TWA (12) and United (5) had added their names to the list and brought the order book up to 82. Aer Lingus, Air India, Delta, Eastern, National, Qantas, SAS and Swissair joined the queue during the course of 1967 and by the time of the first 747's rollout in September 1968, 26 airlines had ordered 158 aircraft. Some of these were for the heavier and longer range 747B (later 747-200) which Boeing was also proposing. This variant would be formally launched in 1968.

It was probably appropriate that the world's largest airliner would be put together in what was the world's largest building, a new facility constructed on 780 acres adjacent to Paine Field at Everett, close to Boeing's other facilities in the Seattle area. Work on the 200 million cubic feet (5.66 million m³) building began immediately the land was acquired in June 1966 and it came on line in May 1967.

Meanwhile, production operations for the 747 began in January 1967 with help from Boeing's other facilities and numerous sub-contractors including Northrop which has long supplied the 747's main fuselage section. Assembly of the first aircraft began in September 1967, a full scale engineering mockup had been completed by January 1968, the first wing was removed from its assembly jig in March 1968, the first body sections were joined in April, the wings and fuselage mated in June and the engines installed in their nacelles in September.

Rollout and First Flight

The first 747, (appropriately registered N7470) was built on production tooling and although owned by Boeing, was regarded as a 747-121, the '21' in the designation suffix indicating Pan Am's customer number. All commercial Boeings since the 707 have used this system, customers retaining the same suffix regardless of the Boeing type involved.

For example, a 747-100 for BOAC/British Airways is a -136, a 747-200 a -236, a 747-400 a -436, a 737-200 a 737-236, a 757-200 a -757-236 and so on. When Boeing ran out of numerical combinations an alpha/numeric system was introduced, resulting in designations like 747-4B5 for a Korean Airlines 747-400.

747 number one was rolled out to considerable fanfare at Boeing's Everett facility on 30 September 1968 in front of a large crowd of dignitaries, workers and invited guests. Painted in the company's new red and white house colours, it carried the logos of the 26 airlines which had placed orders for the revolutionary new transport emblazoned on the forward fuselage. For those present, it was difficult not to be impressed by the size of the aircraft. Most had seen nothing like it before and were in awe.

After that, the 747 was back in the workshop for first flight preparations including activation of its major systems, static testing of the landing gear and flight control systems, fuelling and engine tests and the myriad of other checks that have to be performed.

The big day of first flight finally arrived on 9 February 1969, chief test pilot Jack Waddell, copilot Brien Wygle and flight engineer Jess Wallick lifting the aircraft off at 11.34am on a 1hr 16min maiden sortie which saw them take the aircraft through a series of basic handling and systems trials with the undercarriage locked down. At this stage the aircraft was powered by four JT9D-1s each rated at 42,000lb (186.8kN) thrust.

After touchdown, Waddell described the 747 as "a pilot's dream... the plane handles beautifully."

Then began the eight month, 1,400 hours and 1,013 flights test programme which culminated in FAA certification being awarded on 30 December 1969, a remarkably short time considering the new ground being broken due to the size of the 747. Balancing that was the fact that the 747's basic design principles were largely conservative and proven, utilising many of the philosophies of the 707 only on a larger scale. The wing and control surfaces design, for example, had many similarities with the older aircraft.

Four other 747s were used in the certification programme, these making their first flights in April, May and July (two aircraft) 1969. By the end of that year, eleven 747s were in the air including the first three for TWA. The aircraft's first overseas sortie was on 3 June 1969 when the prototype completed the 4,480nm (8,300km) journey across the Atlantic from Seattle to France to appear at that year's Paris Air Show.

747 Technicalities

The following is an abbreviated description of the 747's major technical characteristics. It applies generally to all 747 models or to specific models where noted:

Fuselage: Conventional semi-monocoque failsafe structure of aluminium alloy skin, circumferential frames and longitudinal stringers; composites used in areas of 747-400 fuselage including main deck floor panels.

Wings: Cantilever construction with aluminium alloy dual path, failsafe structure; thickness/chord ratio 13.44% inboard, 7.8% mid span and 8.0% outboard; dihedral 7deg; incidence 2deg; sweepback 37.5deg at quarter chord; low speed outboard ailerons; high speed inboard ailerons; triple slotted trailing edge flaps; six aluminium honeycomb spoilers per wing (four for flight, two for ground); ten variable camber leading edge flaps outboard and three section Krueger flaps inboard on each wing leading edge; all controls fully powered; advanced aluminium alloys used in wing construction of 747-400 and wingtip extensions with 6ft (1.80in) high swept back winglets fitted.

Tail Surfaces: Cantilever aluminium dual path failsafe structure; variable incidence tailplane with two section elevators; two piece rudder; controls powered.

Undercarriage: Twin forward retracting steerable nosewheel; four 4-wheel main undercarriage bogies under fuselage and wing centre section; anti skid disc brakes on mainwheels; retraction via hydraulic system; steel brakes on 747-100/200/300/SP, carbon brakes on 747-400.

Powerplants: Four Pratt & Whitney, General Electric or Rolls-Royce high by-pass turbofans (see individual models for details). Fuel in wing, fuselage, centre section and tailplane (400 only) tanks; see individual models for capacities.

Systems: Air cycle air conditioning system; max cabin pressure differential 8.9psi (0.61 bar); four independent hydraulic systems each with one engine driven and one pneumatically driven pump, pressure 3,000psi (207 bar); electrical supply via four 60kVA generators (one per engine) on 747-100/200/300/SP (90kVA on 747-400) plus two 60kVA generators on APU for ground operations and emergency supply; gas turbine APU for pneumatic and electrical supplies; 180kVA APU power generation on 747-400; bleed air de-icing system for wing leading edges and engine inlets.

Flight Crew: Two pilots and flight engineer in 747-100/200/300/SP with conventional analogue instruments and avionics; two pilots only in 747-400 with digital avionics and EFIS cockpit.

Stewardesses from the 26 airlines which had ordered 158 747s by the time of its maiden flight pose with the first aircraft. The airlines' logos were applied to both sides of the forward fuselage.

747-100

On 12 December 1969, Pan American took delivery of its first Boeing 747-121, N733PA. This was the sixth aircraft off the line having first flown two months earlier. At this stage the 747 held only provisional certification (the full ticket would be awarded 18 days later), this sufficient to allow the airline to conduct training and route proving activities.

The company's standard initial 'shakedown' flight as it took delivery of each aircraft was from Seattle to New York via Nassau in the Bahamas with most routine familiarisation training conducted from the former US Air Base at Roswell in New Mexico. The first Atlantic crossing by a 747 with a commercial airline crew in charge of the aircraft was conducted on 11 January 1970 when Pan Am's N735PA (number 10 off the line) flew from New York to London as a 'dress rehearsal' for the inaugural service scheduled for 21 January.

As described in the previous chapter, this historic event took place in the early hours of 22 January after a delay caused by technical problems which necessitated a change of aircraft.

Other airlines quickly began receiving 747-100s as 1970 progressed. TWA was the next, receiving its first 747-131 on 31 December 1969 and inaugurating services between Los Angles and New York on 25 February 1970. It introduced international operations (New York-London initially) on 18 March.

Production and deliveries of the 747 built up quickly during 1970 and by the end of the year 85 had been delivered to 17 airlines - Pan Am, TWA, Aer Lingus, Air France, Alitalia, American, BOAC, Continental, Delta, Eastern, Iberia, Japan Air Lines, Lufthansa, National, Northwest, Sabena and United.

Twelve months later another 72 had been delivered and a further 11 airlines added to the list - Air Canada, Air India, Braniff, Condor, El Al, KLM, PAL, Qantas, SAS, South African Airways and Swissair, some of those with the heavier and longer range 747-200B as described in the next chapter.

The 747-100 as initially delivered to the airlines had a maximum takeoff weight of 710,000lb (322,056kg), 30,000lb (13,608kg) more than Boeing had intended. Despite an extensive weight saving programme, increases in structural weight had meant the company found it impossible to meet the lower figure if the promised payload/range performance was to be achieved. Although capable of carrying nearly 500 passengers in a high density single class arrangement, most airlines had two class and quite spacious configurations for around 350 seats, at which load the aircraft in its early form was capable of flying nearly 5,000nm (9,260km) non stop.

Pan Am introduced the 747 to service on 22 January 1970 on the New York-London route. This is 747-121 N747PA *Clipper America*, the second aircraft built and first flown in April 1969.

Perhaps predictably, the introduction of the 747 and its unprecedented passenger carrying capability coincided with the low side of the regular 'end of decade boom/early decade bust' cycle which has affected airlines and airliner manufacturers since World War II. Suddenly, many carriers found themselves with 747s operating at less than 50 per cent load factors, this providing great comfort for the passengers but poor economics for the airlines, which had been investing in the most expensive equipment procurement programmes in their histories.

The result for Boeing was a substantial drop in orders for the 747 - only seven in 1971 and 18 in 1972 - and the need for the manufacturer to dramatically decrease the 747's production rate from the 70-80 per annum in 1970-71 to 30 in 1972 and just 16 in 1975. Since then the production rate has gone up and down under the influence of that cycle, but deliveries have never reached the peak achieved in the first year.

The airlines also had early problems with the 747's Pratt & Whitney JT9D engines to contend with. The 747-100 had originally been planned to have 41,000lb (182.1kN) JT9D-1s when it entered service, this based on the expected 680,000lb (308,448kg) maximum takeoff weight. Although the power of the JT9D-1 could be increased to 42,000lb (186.8kN) by the time the 747 entered service, this was insufficient for the heavier maximum weight and the aircraft entered service with the 43,500lb (193.5kN) JT9D-3 substituted. The JT9D-1 was used only for the flight test programme.

The JT9D-3 was put into service before it was ready and suffered numerous teething problems which resulted in degraded performance and a high unscheduled removal rate. A major problem was caused by a lack of rigidity with the engine-to-pylon mounting system (basically two bolts), the flexing under high loads resulting from this causing the turbine casing to distort (or 'ovalise' as it was called) and make the fan blades rub. Boeing had to design a new engine/pylon interface to correct the problem.

United Airlines 747-122 N4718U *Thomas F Gleed*, delivered to the airline in May 1971. Note the extra top deck windows indicating increased seating in that area.

Sorting this out meant that there were delays in completing aircraft. At one stage in October 1969, as first deliveries were getting close and production was building up, Boeing had rolled out 22 747s of which 17 were sitting on the flight line at Everett awaiting engines. The modified JT9D-3A finally became available later in 1970.

Pratt &Whitney also produced a version of the engine with water injection. As the JT9D-3AW, this produced a greater takeoff thrust of 45,000lb

(200.2kN) which in turn allowed Boeing to offer an optional increased maximum takeoff weight for the 747-100 of 735,000lb (333,396kg). Pan Am modified its early 747-121s by installing this engine and called the aircraft the 747A, an unofficial designation. All members of the basic 747-100 family retained a fuel capacity of 47,210 USgal (178,708 litres) regardless of maximum weight or engine type fitted.

Externally, most 747-100s have three windows per side on the upper deck because as originally certificated, only eight passengers could be carried in that area which was usually configured as a first class lounge. This was subsequently increased to 16 when a smoke barrier was fitted, then 24 if the original spiral staircase was replaced with a straight one and finally 45 when a second emergency exit was installed in combination with the straight stairs.

Those 747-100s with greater seating capacity on the upper deck can be identified by their nine or ten cabin windows per side in that area. Early 747-200Bs also had the eight passengers/three windows upper deck configuration but most were fitted with the larger number of windows.

Some operators chose to modify their 747-100s by having their JT9D-3 engines upgraded to 48,750lb JT9D-7AW standards as the JT9D-7CNW (for 'conversion, water injection'). This was not so much for extra performance but for fleet commonality as airlines began to take delivery of 747-200Bs with 'Dash 7' JT9Ds installed.

747-100: Standard original passenger model as described above with Pratt & Whitney JT9D-3/3A/3AW engines and 710,000lb (322,056kg) or 735,000lb (333,396kg) maximum takeoff weight options. First delivery (to Pan American) 12 December 1969; final delivery (British Airways) April 1976; 166 built.

747-100B: Despite its designation as a '-100 series' 747, the 747-100B was a relatively late addition to the family and first appeared eight years

Another early Pan Am 747-121, N735PA *Clipper Constitution* and the 10th off the line. This 747 was flown from New York to London on 11 January 1970, the first 747 trans-Atlantic crossing with a commercial airline crew and a 'dress rehearsal' for the inaugural scheduled service.

after the (chronologically) second major variant - the 200B - was introduced. Intended as a successor to the original 747-100, the -100B was aimed at those operators who didn't require the additional fuel capacity of the -200B or its substantially increased weights but nevertheless wanted extra operational flexibility through slightly greater weights and a choice of powerplant.

Fundamentally, the 747-100B incorporated a strengthened structure and undercarriage to allow an increased maximum takeoff weight of up to 750,000lb (340,200kg) and was available with either Pratt & Whitney JT9D-7, General Electric GF6-45/50 or Rolls-Royce RB211-524D4 engines of between 48,000lb (213.5kN) and 53,110lb (236.2kN) thrust. Both the CF6 and RB211 had previously been certified for use on the 747-200B in 1975 and 1977, respectively.

Only ten 747-100Bs were built for Iran Air (1) and Saudia (9) with the first example flying on 20 June 1979 and the last delivered in April 1982.

747-100SR: Commonly known as simply the 747SR, this variant was tailored to meet the needs of Japan Air Lines for a large capacity airliner operating over shorter domestic stages than the standard 747-100 and with a much high frequency of takeoffs and landings. The SR is based on the 747-100 airframe and has that version's fuel capacity but was initially offered with much lower maximum takeoff weights of 570,000lb (258,552kg) or 600,000lb (272,160kg). Maximum weights similar to the 747-100B were subsequently made available and customers could choose from the Pratt & Whitney JT9D-7, General Electric CF6-50 or Rolls-Royce RB211-524 families of engines.

BOAC was another early 747 customer, taking delivery of its first aircraft in April 1970. Photographed in its later British Airways colours, this is 747-136 G-AWNN *Sebastian Cabot* during the 1980s.

JAL's SRs were typically configured to carry 498 passengers (16 first class and 482 economy) although in an all economy, high density layout it was possible to carry up to 550 passengers. The 747SR had numerous modifications to suit its high frequency, short range operations including heavier duty tyres, wheels and brakes (the latter with fan cooling), a modified pressurisation system and some structural modifications.

JAL ordered its first of 12 JT9D powered SRs in October 1972 and inaugurated services on its Tokyo-Okinawa route 12 months later, the first aircraft having flown on 4 September 1973. The only other SR customer was All Nippon Airways, which received the first of 17 with CF6s in December 1978. The 29th and last 747-100SR was delivered to ANA in November 1982.

BOEING 747-100

Powerplants: Initially four 43,500lb (193.5kN) Pratt & Whitney JT9D-3/3A turbofans then a choice of 45,000lb (200.2kN) JT9D-3AW; 46,950lb (208.8kN) JT9D-7A; 48,000lb (213.5kN) JT9D-7F; 46,500lb (206.8kN) General Electric CF6-45A2; 52,500lb (233.5kN) CF6-50E2 or 53,110lb (236.2kN) Rolls-Royce RB211-524D4 turbofans. Fuel capacity 47,210 USgal (178,708 l).

Dimensions: Wing span 195ft 8in (59.64m); length 231ft 10in (70.66m); height 63ft 5in (19.33m); wing area 5,500sq ft (510.9m²); wheelbase 84ft 0in (25.60m); wheel track 36ft 1in (11.00m).

Weights: Operating empty 373,500-378,900lb (169,420-171,869kg); max takeoff 710,000lb (322,056kg), 735,000lb (333,396kg) or 750,000lb (340,200kg); max zero fuel 526,500lb (238,820kg); max payload 147,600-153,000lb (66,950-69,400kg)

Accommodation: Typically 366 passengers in three classes or up to 442 in single class ten abreast; high density arrangement for up to 550 passengers in 747-100SR. Main cabin length 187ft 0in (57.00m); max width 20ft 1¹/₂in (6.13m); max height 8ft 4in (2.54m); passenger deck volume 27,860cu ft (788.9m³); under-floor baggage holds volume 5,190cu ft (147.0m³).

Performance: Max cruise 522kt (967km/h); economical cruise 490kt (907km/h); operational ceiling 45,000ft (13,716m); range with 442 passengers 4,500nm (8,335km); range with 366 passengers 5,500nm (10,187km).

747-200

Heavier, more powerful and longer range versions of the 747 with additional fuel capacity had figured early in Boeing's long term planning for the aircraft, as did convertible and pure freighter versions. Originally designated 747B (passenger), 747C (convertible) and 747F (freighter), these were subsequently grouped together under the overall designation 747-200 as the -200B, -200C and -200F, respectively. A mixed passenger/freight variant, the 747-200M Combi was later added to the line.

Formally announced in November 1968 but able to be ordered before then, the 747-200 was based around the planned availability of the 45,500lb (202.4kN) thrust Pratt & Whitney JT9D-7 engine and then the 47,900lb (213.0kN) JT9D-7W with water injection.

Many airlines opted to wait for the 747-200B rather than purchase the shorter range -100 and by the time of the first 747's maiden flight in February 1969, 11 of them (Air India, Air Portugal, Alitalia, El Al, Iberia, JAL, KLM, Qantas, SAS, South African Airways and Swissair) had placed orders for the heavier version. Of these, Alitalia, Iberia and JAL had also ordered 747-100s.

The 747-200B differed from its predecessor in having structural and undercarriage modifications to allow greater operating weights, more powerful engines and additional fuel capacity in the wings giving a total of 51,430 USgal (194,683 l). Extended range tanks in the outer wings were offered optionally, that and some rejigging of the main tanks bringing the -200B's maximum fuel capacity up to 53,985 USgal (204,355 l). Overall dimensions remained as before as did the aircraft's systems and its accommodation options.

As originally delivered, the 747-200B had a maximum takeoff weight of 775,000lb (351,540kg). With increases in power available from upgraded versions of the JT9D and the General Electric CF6 and Rolls-Royce RB211 which later became available, this was increased in optional steps to ultimately 833,000lb (377,849kg). With 442 passengers on board in a typical two class layout a 747-200B could fly about 700nm (1,296km) further than a -100; with 366 passengers in three classes the advantage increased by up to 1,400nm (2,593km).

The first 747-200B (line number 88) flew on 11 October 1970, FAA certification was awarded on 23 December and the initial delivery was to KLM on 16 January 1971. In November 1970, one of the first 747-200Bs set a new world record for weight when it took off at a gross mass of 820,700lb (372,269kg).

The 747-200 introduced increased weights, greater range and powerplant options and was always part of Boeing's planning for a 'family' of 747s. CP Air's C-FCRA *Empress of Asia* was delivered in November 1973 as the 225th 747 off the line.

Airlines were given more powerplant options as the 1970s progressed, the first alternative to the JT9D being the General Electric CF6. The prototype 747 was re-engined with 51,000lb (226.8kN) thrust CF6-50Ds and reflown in its new form on 26 June 1973. For a short time, it was planned to market the CF6 powered aircraft as the 747-300, but this was dropped.

The first customer for the 747-200 with CF6 engines was the US Air Force for its E-4 airborne command post aircraft (see 'Military 747s' section), an initial order for three being placed in February 1973. The first airline customer was KLM, which ordered CF6 powered 747-200M Combis in July 1974. Deliveries began in October 1975.

The Rolls-Royce RB211 option took a bit longer to materialise. British Airways wanted to standardise on the engine as its Lockheed TriStars were similarly powered. The RB211-524s used in the TriStars were rated at 48,000lb (213.5kN) thrust, about 2,000lb (8.9kN) less than was required for the 747.

Development of the uprated RB211-524B required British Government backing but this was withheld for over a year from April 1974 while awaiting a second customer so as to minimise the commercial risk. Approval was finally given in June 1975 on the basis of an initial British Airways order for only four, although others soon followed.

The 747-200 Combi provided operators with the flexibility to carry either passengers, freight or a combination of the two. CAAC's 747-2J6 Combi B-2446 was delivered in December 1983.

The flight deck of an early 747 reflects the available technology of the time and contrasts greatly with the digital 747-400 cockpit illustrated later. The flight engineer's station can just be seen in the lower right of the picture.

Some early 747-200Bs (such as this JAL 747-246B JA8113) had the smaller upper deck area and therefore only three windows per side in that area. The 192nd 747, it was delivered in June 1972.

Braniff became well known for its garish colour schemes during the 1970s. This particular 747-227B (N605BN) intended for the airline was flown in March 1980 wearing appropriate titles but was not delivered, remaining in storage until sold to Northwest in 1984.

The Rolls-Royce RB211 and General Electric CF6 became available as engine options for the 747 in the mid 1970s. Cathay Pacific's VR-HKG has RB211s and was delivered to the airline in July 1979.

The first RB211 powered 747 (a -236B for British Airways) was flown in September 1976 and initial delivery was in June 1977. In November 1976 this aircraft set a new weight-to-height record when took off at a gross weight of 840,500lb (381,250kg) and climbed to a an altitude of 6,562ft (2,000m) in 6min 33sec.

A General Electric CF6 powered 747-271C operated by UTA on lease from Transamerica Airlines.

747-200B: Passenger version as described above; first flight 11 October 1970, first delivery to KLM 16 January 1971 and final delivery (to Air China) October 1990; 226 built.

747-200F: If the standard versions of the 747 were responsible for a revolution in air transport's passenger carrying activities, so was the dedicated freighter, this making a very high capacity and long range cargo carrier readily available to commercial operators for the first time. As had been the case with the passenger 747, the freighter's operating economics took it into new areas of commercial possibilities.

Compared to the passenger version, the 747-200F featured a nose loading door hinged just below the flight deck (allowing it to swing upwards for clear access to the main deck), an optional 11ft 2in x 10ft 0in (3.40m x 3.05m) upwards opening cargo door on the port side rear fuselage, two starboard side lower lobe cargo doors (fore and aft of the wing), a mechanised cargo handling system which allowed two operators to load a full payload in 30 minutes, a strengthened main deck floor, cabin windows removed and structural modifications which allowed an increase in maximum zero fuel weight to 590,000lb (267,624kg).

This resulted in a maximum payload of up to 247,800lb (112,402kg), a typical load comprising 29 10ft 0in x 8ft 0in x 8ft 0in (3.05m x 2.44m x 2.44m) containers on the main deck plus 30 173cu ft (4.90m^3) containers in the lower lobe. The 747-200F's payload-range performance meant that 200,000lb (90,720kg) could be carried more than 4,500nm (8,335km).

The first 747-200F (line number 168) was flown on 30 November 1971, certification was awarded on 7 March 1972 and the aircraft delivered to Lufthansa two days later. New 747-200Fs were subsequently also delivered to Air China, Air France, British Airways, Cargolux, Cathay Pacific, China Airlines, El Al, Flying Tiger, the Imperial Iranian Air Force, JAL, Nippon Cargo, Northwest, Pan American, Saudia, Seaboard World, Singapore Airlines and UTA for a total of 76 aircraft. The last 747-200 variant of any kind to be delivered was an F to Nippon Cargo in November 1991.

747-200C: Convertible model with the ability to be converted from all passenger to all freight configuration in about 24 hours or to a mixture of passenger/cargo layouts with passengers forward and freight aft.

The 747-200F had a significant effect on commerce because for the first time, a high capacity and long range freighter was available to the airlines. Cargolux's 747-2R7F LX-DCV *City of Luxembourg* was delivered in January 1979.

The 747-200C featured the upwards hinging nose loading door, strengthened fuselage and main deck floor, cargo handling system and optional cargo door on the port side rear fuselage of the 747-200F. Maximum weight and engine options were as per the 747-200B. The 747-200C first flew on 23 March 1973 and deliveries to World Airways began the following month. Production was sporadic with only 13 built for El Al (2), Iraqi Airways (3), Martinair Holland (2), Transamerica (3) and World (3). The last example was handed over to Martinair in September 1988.

747-200M Combi: The Combi version of the 747-200 featured the port side rear fuselage cargo door and a slightly increased maximum zero fuel weight of 545,000lb (247,2123kg). Either all passenger, all freight or a combination of the two could be carried with passengers forward and freight aft in the mixed configuration.

The first 747 Combi was converted from a Sabena 747-100 and after modification was redelivered to the airline in February 1974. The first production 747-200M (line number 250) was flown on 18 November 1974 and delivered to Air Canada in March 1975. Other customers were Air China, Air France, Air Gabon, Air Madagascar, Alitalia, Avianca, British Airways, CAAC, Cameroon Airlines, China Airlines, Iberia, Iran Air, KLM, Kuwait Airways, Lufthansa, Middle East Airlines, Pakistan International, Royal Air Maroc, Royal Jordanian, SAS, South African Airways, UTA and Varig for a total of 78 aircraft.

Classic Upgrades

The early model 747-100/200 'Classics' have been subject to several upgrade programmes including conversion to freighters. Some of those which have been performed or were planned by mid 2000 are listed below:

Boeing Freighter Conversion: Boeing began investigating a freighter conversion programme for the 747-100/200 passenger models as early as 1972 with the first one completed in 1974. Nearly 80 had been performed for 45 customers by 2000. The conversion is similar to the 'Large Cargo Door' programme noted below, and like that and other freighter conversions, does not involve installing the 747-200F's nose loading door. Optional increased maximum zero fuel and landings weights are offered along with maximum takeoff weight options up to 833,000lb (377,849kg).

Boeing Large Cargo Door: Instigated by Boeing in the early 1980s, this programme involved fitting the large port side rear fuselage cargo door, strengthened main deck floor, mechanised cargo handling system to 747-100s and -200s. Weight increases were also offered and pure freighter, convertible and Combi options were available.

Boeing Military Airplanes modified 19 Pan American 747s to this standard (as passenger/freight convertibles) to support the US Air Force's Civil Reserve Air Fleet (CRAF) for which they were given the military designation

C-19A. The first modified 747 was redelivered to Pan Am in May 1985 and the last in February 1990.

Boeing PMS: The Performance Management System (PMS) was developed jointly by Boeing and Delco and is based around a computer with its memory programmed with the operator's economic information and performance data for the individual aircraft. The PMS receives airspeed, altitude, fuel flow, wind, air temperature and other data during flight and automatically calculates the optimum airspeeds, power settings, attitude and other information for the aircraft so it can be flown for minimum fuel burn and/or minimum operating costs. The first system was delivered in June 1982.

Pemco 747-100 Cargo Conversion: Aircraft fitted with large rear fuselage freight door, strengthened main deck floor, blanked off windows and electric cargo handling system. An ex TWA 747-100 was the first aircraft converted and certification was awarded in April 1988. Five additional aircraft have since been converted.

IAI 747-100/200 Freighter Conversion: Basically similar to other freighter conversions with large cargo door on port side, reinforced floor, local fuselage strengthening and powered ball mat/roller cargo handling system. First conversion (a 747-100) certificated in 1990, customers include Lufthansa (6), South African Airways (1), Polaris (7), Air France (1) and KLM (2).

HAECO 747-200 Freighter Conversion: The HAECO (Hong Kong Aircraft Engineering Company Ltd) programme was launched in November 1995 with an order from Atlas Air to convert 10 747-200M Combis to full freighter configuration.

Upgraded Cockpit: Boeing and Honeywell announced in April 2000 they had developed a 'glass cockpit' upgrade for 747 Classics based on a simple replacement of the primary flight instruments with four Honeywell flat panel displays for primary flight and navigation information. The flight engineer's station would be retained but the new cockpit would have a dual type rating with the 747-400.

At the same time, Boeing Airplane Services announced it was looking at a programme to install a modern panel in 747-100/200/300s and convert the cockpit to a two pilot configuration without a flight engineer.

Winglets: Aviation Partners and Boeing began flight testing of a 747-200F fitted with 14ft 6in (4.42m) high carbon fibre blended winglets in mid 2000. The winglets were expected to yield a 5-7 per cent improvement in specific fuel consumption and enhanced hot and high performance.

One of several early model 747 freighter conversions is that performed by Israeli Aircraft Industry's Bedek Aviation division. This is the former Air France 747-128 F-BPVC, originally built in 1970 and converted to a freighter by IAI in 1992.

The former Cargolux 747-2R7F LX-DCV (as illustrated previously) later in its career as Federal Express's N639FE. Federal Express began leasing the aircraft in 1989 - this photograph was taken in 1996.

BOEING 747-200

Powerplants: Four 47,900lb (213.0kN) Pratt & Whitney JT9D-7W; 54,750lb (243.5kN) JT9D-7R4G2; 52,500lb (233.5kN) General Electric CF6-50E2; 56,700lb (252.2kN) CF6-80C2B1 or 53,110lb (236.2kN) Rolls-Royce RB211-524D4 turbofans. Max fuel capacity 53,985 USgal (204,355 l).

Dimensions: Wing span 195ft 8in (59.64m); length 231ft 10in (70.66m); height 63ft 5in (19.33m); wing area 5,500sq ft (510.9m²).

Weights: 200B - operating empty 374,700-383,600lb (169,964-174,000kg); max takeoff 775,000lb (351,540kg), 785,000lb (356,076kg), 800,000lb (362,880kg), 820,000lb (371,952kg) or 833,000lb (377,849kg); max landing 564,000-630,000lb (255,830-285,768kg); max zero fuel 526,000lb (238,594kg); max payload 142,400-151,300lb (64,592-68,630kg). 200F - max takeoff options as for 200B; max zero fuel 590,000lb (267,624kg); max payload 38,900-247,800lb (108,365-112,402kg).

Accommodation: 200B - typically 366-397 passengers in three classes, 452 passengers in two classes or up to 516 passengers single class high density ten abreast. 200F - total cargo volume 24,260cu ft (687.0m³).

Performance: 200B - max cruise 522-530kt (967-982km/h); economical cruise 490kt (907km/h); cruise ceiling 45,000ft (13,716m); range with 366 passengers 6,350-6,900nm (11,762-12,780km) depending on engine and maximum weight option; range with 442 passengers 5,200nm (9,630km); 200F - range with 200,000lb (90,720kg) payload 4,550-4,900nm (8,428-9,076km).

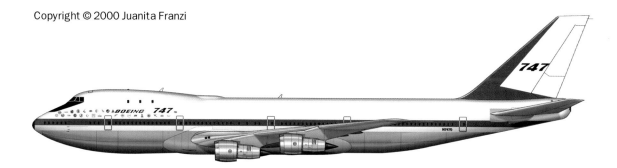

The first 747 (N7470, c/n 20235, l/n 1) at the time of its maiden flight 9 February 1969.

Pan Am 747-121 N736PA (c/n 19643, l/n 11) *Clipper Victor* temporarily renamed *Clipper Young America* for inaugural New York-London flight 22 January 1970.

British Airways 747-236B G-BDXI *City of Cambridge*, c/n 21830, l/n 430.

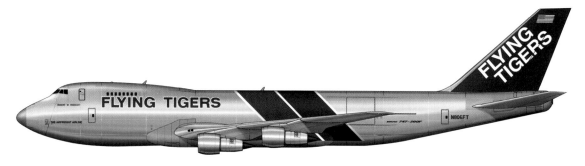

Flying Tiger Line 747-249F N806FT *Robert W Prescott* c/n 21827, l/n 406).

Qantas 747SP-38 VH-EAA *City Of Gold Coast Tweed*, c/n 22495, l/n 505.

US Air Force VC-25A (747-2G4B) 82-8000, c/n 23824, l/n 679.

Singapore Airlines 747-312 N119KE, c/n 23030, l/n 593.

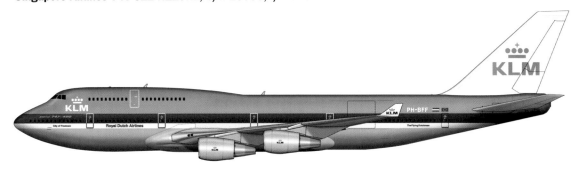

KLM 747-406M Combi PH-BFF *City of Freetown*, c/n 24202, l/n 770.

747SP

A long range version of the 747 developed to meet a requirement for non stop long haul sectors such as New York-Tokyo, New York-Dhahran and Los Angeles-Sydney, the SP ('Special Performance') swapped payload for additional range with its fuselage shortened by 14.35m (47ft 1in) compared to other 747 models with a resultant reduction in passenger capacity. The vertical tail surfaces were enlarged (and fitted with a double hinged rudder) to compensate for the shorter fuselage and a lightened structure was incorporated in parts of the wing, fuselage and landing gear.

Maximum weights were reduced (although several options were offered up to a maximum of 700,000lb/317,520kg) and redesigned trailing edge wing flaps plus new wing/body fairings and leading edge fillets were fitted. Maximum fuel capacity was the same as the 747-200B and the SP's smaller fuselage reduced empty weight by about 50,000lb (22,680kg). The SP retained about 90 per cent commonality with the 747-100/200 models in terms of spare parts and maintenance requirements and offered flight crew interchangeability with the larger aircraft.

The first 747SP flew on 4 July 1975, certification was awarded in February 1976 and Pan American took delivery of the first of 10 it would eventually receive the following month.

Despite its impressive range capabilities, the SP was a relatively slow seller for Boeing as it appealed to a largely niche market. Most of the 14 customers took delivery of only twos and threes as supplements to their main fleets. Compared to the 747-200, the SP achieved a lower fuel burn and trip costs were about 14 per cent less, although seat-mile costs were greater due to its lower seating capacity. Airfield performance was unequalled by any other 747, especially in hot and high conditions, the SP requiring only about three-quarters of the runway length needed for takeoff by a 747-200.

The 747SP achieved its main purpose - to be capable of flying hitherto untapped non stop long haul routes - and pioneered several including New York-Tokyo, Sydney-San Francisco, Taipei-Los Angeles and Hong Kong-San Francisco. A couple were sold as long range VIP transports for Heads of State.

The 747SP also set several long distance records in the mid 1970s, the most prominent of which was on the delivery flight of a South African

The short fuselage 747SP swapped carrying capacity for longer range and set several distance records in its early days. 747SP-21 N40135 illustrated here in Boeing 'house' colours first flew in November 1975 and was delivered to Pan American as N533PA *Clipper Freedom* four months later.

Fourteen operators between them ordered the modest total of 45 747SPs with deliveries stretching from March 1976 to December 1989. China's CAAC received four 747SP-J6s from February 1980.

Airways aircraft on 23-24 March 1976. With 50 passengers on board, it flew nonstop from Paine Field in Washington State to Cape Town, a distance of 8,940nm (16,560km). This was a world record for a commercial aircraft and only beaten 13 years later when a Qantas 747-400 flew 9,688nm (17,945km) nonstop from England to Australia on its delivery flight. In October 1977 a Pan Am SP set a new speed record for an around the world flight passing over both poles, covering 23,208nm (42,9780km) in 54hr 7min 12 sec.

Apart from Pan Am, other customers for the SP were South African Airways (6), the Abu Dhabi Government (1), Braniff (3), China's CAAC (4), China Airlines (4), Iran Air (4), Iraqi Airways (1), Korean Air Lines (2), Qantas (2), the Saudi Government (1), Saudia (2), Syrian Arab Airlines (2) and TWA (3). The 45th and final SP was delivered to Abu Dhabi in December 1989.

BOEING 747SP

Powerplants: Four 46,500lb (206.8kN) General Electric CF6-45A2 or -50E2F; 46,250lb (205.7kN) Pratt & Whitney JT9D-7A; 50,100lb (222.8kN) Rolls-Royce RB211-524B2; 51,600lb (229.5kN) RB211-524C2 or 53,110lb (236.2kN) RB211-524D4 turbofans. Fuel capacity 50,359 USgal (190,629 l).

Dimensions: Wing span 195ft 8in (59.64m); length 184ft 9in (56.31m); height 65ft 5in (19.94m); wing area 5,500sq ft (510.9m²); wheelbase 67ft 4in (20.52m).

Weights: Operating empty 333,900lb (151,457kg); max takeoff 630,000lb (285,768kg), 660,000lb (299,376kg), 670,000lb (303,912kg), 690,000lb (312,984kg), 696,000lb (315,705kg) or 700,000lb (317,520kg); max landing 450,000-465,000lb (204,120-210,924kg); max zero fuel 410,000-450,000lb (185,976-204,120kg); max payload 76,100-91,100lb (34,519-41,277kg).

Accommodation: Typically 276-316 passengers in two classes or maximum of 440 in single class ten abreast. Main cabin length 138ft 8in (42.26m); main cabin volume 21,660cu ft (613.3m³); underfloor baggage holds volume 3,460cu ft (98.0m³).

Performance: Max speed 538kt (996km/h); service ceiling 45,100ft (13,746m); range with 276 passengers 6,650nm (12,318km); range with 331 passengers 5,200nm (9,632km); max ferry range 8,000nm (14,818km).

747-300

The 747-300 introduced the first increase in cabin area to the 747 by incorporating a stretched upper deck capable of accommodating up to 69 economy class passengers. It resulted from a number of Boeing studies which looked at increasing the aircraft's seating capacity, these starting even before the first aircraft had flown.

Ideas examined included fuselage plugs fore and aft of the wing to allow an increase in seating to around 600. These early ideas were thwarted thanks to the cyclic nature of the airline industry, which hit the bottom of the graph in the early 1970s when 747 orders and production declined rapidly after the initial rush. Boeing therefore temporarily dropped plans for a 747 with increased seating capacity.

The market began to pick up in the second half of the decade, prompting Boeing to take another look a higher capacity 747. Once again, a fuselage stretch and seating capacity of around 600 were examined, as was the idea of extending the upper deck over the whole length of the fuselage to create a full 'double decker' 747 capable of carrying over 700 passengers.

Once again, a low point of the airline cycle hit, Boeing finally announcing a more conservative version initially known as the 747SUD (Stretched Upper Deck) in June 1980 following a launch order for five from Swissair. This designation was soon changed to 747EUD (for Extended Upper Deck), and then to 747-300. It has been noted that the 747-300 was the first 'nine figure' airliner; that is each one cost more than $US100,000,000.

Better utilising the upper deck for increased passenger accommodation had seen an evolutionary process in the 747-100 and -200. As it was initially certificated, only eight passengers could be carried in that area (which was therefore regarded as a first class lounge) but it was subsequently increased to 16 with the installation of a smoke barrier, then 24 if the original spiral staircase between the decks was replaced with a straight one, and finally 45 when a second emergency exit was fitted in combination with the straight staircase. With the spiral stairs retained, the new limit was 32.

Compared to the 747-200, the -300's upper deck was stretched aft by 7.11m (23ft 4in), increasing the maximum possible economy class seating in the area to 69 six abreast. The lengthened upper deck featured two new emergency exit doors and allowed the fitting of an optional crew rest area immediately behind the flight deck.

Maximum takeoff weight, fuel and powerplant options were the same as the -200, this in combination with a heavier empty weight resulting in a marginally inferior payload-range performance, but by way of compensation

The 747-300 (originally SUD - 'stretched upper deck' or EUD - 'extended upper deck') was the first variant to introduce an increase in cabin area. Swissair was the launch customer, ordering five in June 1980 and taking delivery of its first in March 1983.

the new extended upper decking produced a reduction in drag which resulted in 10-11 per cent lower fuel consumption per passenger.

The extended upper deck was also offered by Boeing as a retrofit to existing 747-100/200s (which would be redesignated as -300s), the eight week conversion involving removing a 95ft (29m) section of the upper fuselage from immediately behind the flight deck and slotting in the new sections. The only airline to take up this option was KLM, which had 10 aircraft modified. The airline subsequently converted two of these to freighters, creating the first all cargo 747s with the stretched upper deck

The first 747-300 flew on 5 October 1982 (with Pratt &Whitney JT9D engines) and the second (with General Electric CF6s) on 10 December 1982. First deliveries were to launch customer Swissair and UTA (which ordered three) in March 1983. Other customers were Air India (2), Cathay Pacific (6), Egyptair (2), International Lease Finance Corporation (3), Japan Asia Airways (1), Japan Air Lines (13), Korean Air Lines (3), KLM (3), Malaysia Airlines (1), Qantas (6), Sabena (2), Saudia (10), Singapore Airlines (14), South African Airways (2), Thai International (2), UTA (3) and Varig (2).

Several of these opted for the 747-300M Combi with the large cargo door on the port side fuselage aft of the wing (sometimes in combination with the standard model), while the -300SR version optimised for short stage lengths and was purchased only by Japan Air Lines.

In hindsight, it can be argued that the 747-300 was very much an interim higher capacity version of the 747 pending the introduction of the more advanced -400 (with its 'second generation' high bypass engines and greater range), production amounting to a relatively modest 81 examples.

The last one (a Combi) was delivered to Sabena in September 1990. Four months earlier, Boeing had announced that the -400 would be the only 747 model offered to the marketplace from that point.

747-300: Standard passenger version, first delivery to Swissair in March 1983, 56 built.

747-300M Combi: Mixed passenger/freight model with cargo door on rear port fuselage and increased maximum zero fuel weight and payload; typical mixed load 289 passengers and seven pallets; first delivery to UTA in March 1983, 21 built.

France's UTA took delivery of three 747-300s from March 1983 including two Combis. This is 747-3B3 F-GDUA, the 573rd 747 off the line.

747-300SR: Specialised variant for Japanese high frequency and short range domestic operations with lower maximum weights and accommodation for a theoretical maximum of 624 passengers in a very high density layout; four built for Japan Air Lines and delivered from December 1987.

747-300 Special Freighter: Work on three conversions of 747-300s to freight-

Stretched Upper Deck Combi

17% INCREASE IN PASSENGERS
RELATIVE TO STANDARD BODY

ers began in May 2000 against an order from Atlas Air. The conversions will be performed by Boeing's Wichita facility, the company hoping they will be the first of a number of stretched upper deck (SUD) 747 freighter conversions including for the -400. The 747-300 'Special Freighter' will be able to carry a 235,000lb (106,595kg) payload over a range of 4,200nm (7,770km).

Sectional drawing of the 'Stretched Upper Deck' (747-300M) Combi showing a typical mixed load and the large cargo door on the rear fuselage. Boeing built 21 747-300Ms, the first one delivered to UTA in March 1983.

BOEING 747-300

Powerplants: Four 54,750lb (243.5kN) Pratt & Whitney JT9D-7R4G2; 53,110lb (236.2kN) Rolls-Royce RB211-524D4; 52,500lb (233.5kN) General Electric CF6-50E2 or 56,700lb (252.2kN) CF6-80C2B1 turbofans. Max fuel capacity 53,985 USgal (204,355 l).

Dimensions: Wing span 195ft 8in (59.64m); length 231ft 10in (70.66m); height 63ft 5in (19.33m); wing area 5,500sq ft (510.9m²).

Weights: Operating empty 383,900-396,000lb (174,137-179,625kg); max takeoff 775,000lb (351,540kg), 785,000lb (356,076kg), 800,000lb (362,880kg), 820,000lb (371,952kg) or 833,000lb (377,848kg); max landing 574,000-630,000lb (260,366-285,768kg); max zero fuel 300 - 535,000lb (242,676kg), 300M - 565,000lb (256,284kg); max payload 300 - 142,200-151,100lb (64,502-68,539kg), 300M - 169,000-177,900lb (76,658-80,695kg).

Accommodation: Typically 400 passengers in three classes or 470 in two classes.

Performance: Max cruise 507kt (939km/h); economical cruise 490kt (907km/h); long range cruise 485kt (898km/h); range with 400 passengers 6,100-6,700nm (11,300-12,410km) depending on powerplant and maximum weight option.

747-400

In May 1985, Boeing announced it was developing an advanced, longer range version of the 747-300 which promised greater efficiency and lower operating costs. This was achieved by combining 'second generation' Pratt & Whitney PW4000, General Electric CF6-80 or Rolls-Royce RB211-524G engines in the 58,000-60,000lb (258.0-266.9kN) thrust class with refined aerodynamics, a two crew digital flight deck (with no flight engineer), structural modifications, additional fuel capacity, increased maximum takeoff weight options and numerous other refinements.

The result was the 747-400, an aircraft which could carry more people faster and further than previous models. The company estimated the new aircraft would consume up to 12 per cent less fuel per passenger than the 747-300 and up to 24 per cent less than the -200. Boeing quoted a fuel burn of 300lb (136kg) per passenger on a 3,000nm (5,557km) journey for the 747-400 compared to 409lb (185kg) per passenger for the 747-100.

Typically configured, the 747-400 was able to fly up to 1,100nm (2,035km) further than the -300, this capability opening up the possibility of new non stop city pairings for operators including New York-Seoul, Singapore-London, Los Angeles-Sydney, London-Tokyo and Hong Kong-Los Angeles.

Externally, the 747-400 retained the -300's fuselage with extended upper deck but there were major changes to the wings, each of which featured a 6ft 0in (1.83m) tip extension to which was added a 6ft 0in (1.83m) winglet canted outboard at an angle of 22deg and swept back 60deg. The drag reduction provided by the winglets produced a 3 per cent increase in range. The internal structure of the wings was also modified, incorporating advanced aluminium alloys developed for the Boeing 757 and 767 and resulting in a weight saving of around 6,000lb (2,722kg).

More weight was cut through the use of carbon instead of steel brakes, these in combination with wider wheels and low profile tyres providing an 1,800lb (816kg) saving in the undercarriage. Floor panels made of graphite composite instead of metal also contributed to the weight reduction, while a

The first 747-400, a PW4056 powered 747-451 destined for Northwest Airlines, first flew on 29 April 1988 as N401PW. It was the 696th aircraft off the line and after being used for development work was delivered to Northwest as N661US in December 1989.

reprofiled wing-to-body fairing and redesigned engines and mounting pylons also resulted in reduced drag.

The basic capacity of the 747-400's main wing and centre section fuel tanks remained the same as the -300 at 53,985 USgal (204,355 litres) but this could be increased to 57,285 USgal (216,847 litres) with an optional 3,300 USgal (12,492 litres) in the horizontal tail surfaces, the tanks located between the front and rear spars. This provided an extra 350nm (648nm) range.

The completely redesigned two pilot cockpit was - despite the lack of a flight engineer - intended to reduce crew workload with second generation digital avionics based around six 8 x 8in (20.3 x 20.3cm) cathode ray tube (CRT) primary displays. Boeing liked to show the difference between this modern cockpit and the old 'dials, bells and whistles' style of arrangement by pointing out that the 747-100/200/300 models' 971 lights, gauges and switches were reduced to only 365 in the new model.

Inside, the 747-400 introduced larger overhead stowage bins, modular galley and toilet designs, greater cabin configuration flexibility and an upgraded entertainment system providing a larger number of channels from which passengers could choose. To cater for the very long flights the 747-400 was capable of performing, a crew rest area could be installed.

The 747-400 was launched in October 1985 with the announcement of an order from Northwest and by the time the first development aircraft (powered by PW4056 engines) flew on 29 April 1988, a further 15 airlines (Air France, Air New Zealand, All Nippon Airways, British Airways, Cathay Pacific, China Airlines, JAL, KLM, Korean Air Lines, Lufthansa, Qantas, Singapore Airlines, Thai International, United and UTA) plus the Japanese Government had added their names to the orderbook.

US certification (with PW4056s) was awarded in January 1989 and the first delivery was made to Northwest later in the same month. Certification of the GE CF6-80C2 powered 747-400 was awarded in May 1989 and that of the Rolls-Royce RB211-524G version in June 1989. In August 1989 the

The 747-400 represented a substantial advance over the previous versions. Singapore Airlines took delivery of more than 50 from March 1989 and called them 'Megatop', a natural progression from the 'Big Top' name given to its 747-300s.

(Opposite) The 747-400 two crew cockpit is vastly different from the 'Classic' models (see earlier illustration) with a considerably reduced number of gauges, lights and switches. The cathode ray tube displays are well shown here.

(Above) A general view of the 747-400 production line with Japan Air Lines' 75th 747 starting to take shape in the foreground. JAL has so far ordered 111 747s in all major series except the SP.

first 747-400 for Qantas flew 9,688nm (17,945km) non stop from London to Sydney on its delivery flight, a new world distance record for a commercial aircraft. The previous mark of 8,940nm (16,560km) was set in March 1976 by a South African Airways 747SP flying between Seattle and Cape Town. The Qantas 747 was powered by Rolls-Royce engines.

The -400 has since gone on to become by far the best selling of all the 747 models and operated by most of the world's international airlines. By May 2000, 592 had been sold (45 per cent of the total orderbook) of which 517 had been delivered.

Marketing of the earlier 747 versions ended in May 1990 in favour of the -400 family. The 747-100/200/SP/300 models were subsequently referred to by the company as the 747 'Classics'.

747-400: Standard passenger version as described above; first flight 29 April 1988, first delivery (to Northwest) January 1989; 436 ordered by May 2000.

747-400M: Combi mixed passenger/freight version with 11 ft 2in x 10ft 0in (5.06m x 3.05m) cargo door on port side rear fuselage and flexible interior options, a typical layout being 266 passengers in three classes in the front of the cabin and six or seven pallets to the rear weighing up to 60,000lb (27,216kg). With no freight aboard the Combi can carry up to 413 passengers.

The first 747-400M order was placed by KLM in April 1986 and initial delivery to the same airline was in September 1989. A total of 63 had been ordered by May 2000 for 14 operators, most of them using the Combi to supplement their 747-400 passenger aircraft fleets.

747-400D: 'Domestic' - a special high capacity version developed for high frequency short range services, and like the 747-100SR intended mainly for the Japanese market. The 747-400D combines the -400's fuselage with a strengthened wing which lacks the other -400 versions' tip extensions and winglets. It is available only with Pratt & Whitney or General Electric engines.

Other modifications for the -400D's operations include a strengthened upper deck floor, five extra upper deck windows, some local fuselage reinforcement, brake cooling fans and revised pressurisation system. The extended tips and winglets can be added if the aircraft is used for long range operations. The 747-400D has a typical passenger capacity of 566 in a high density, two class arrangement and the standard maximum takeoff weight is substantially reduced to 600,000lb (272,160kg). Range with 566 passengers is 1,720nm (3,185km).

The 747-400D has been ordered by Japan Air Lines (8) and All Nippon Airways (11) with the first example delivered to JAL in October 1991.

747-400F: The dedicated freighter version combining the upwards opening nose cargo door, side cargo doors and fuselage of the 747-200F (including its short upper deck and strengthened main deck floor) with the stronger wings of the 747-400 complete with extended tips and winglets.

Powerplant and maximum weight options are as per the passenger 747-400 but the maximum zero fuel weight is increased from 535,000lb (242,676kg) to 610,000lb (276,696kg) if the higher maximum takeoff weights are specified. Maximum landing weight can also be increased under the same conditions. An improved version of the 747-200F's freight handling system is incorporated.

Applying spectacular and arty colour schemes to 747s (and other airliners) has become popular in recent times. Qantas 747-438 VH-OJB *Wunala Dreaming* **was one of the pioneering examples, the Aboriginal design creating interest wherever it went.**

(Opposite) 747-400F HL-7419 of Asiana Cargo with its 'mouth' open, showing the nose loading door to good effect. This particular aircraft - the 1044ᵗʰ off the line - was delivered in November 1994.

The first 747-400F freighter in Boeing livery. It first flew in May 1993 and the 'house' registration N6005C was one often used by the manufacturer. It was temporarily applied to some 30 747s before handover. This N6005C is a 747-428F intended for delivery to Air France as F-GIUA but not taken up, the aircraft going into storage.

The 747-400F can carry a payload of up to 273,350lb (124,000kg) over a range of between 3,200nm (5,925km) and 4,450nm (8,240km) depending on the powerplant and maximum weight option. Main deck volume is 21,347cu ft ($604.5m^3$) with an additional 5,600cu ft ($158.6m^3$) available in the underfloor holds. The main deck can carry 30 pallets and 32 LD1 containers plus bulk cargo can be accommodated in the underfloor holds.

The first 747-400F flew on 7 May 1993 and the first delivery was to Cargolux in November 1993; total of 74 ordered for 11 customers by May 2000.

747-400 PIP: 'Performance Improvement Package' - announced on April 1993, the 747-400 PIP was introduced in two stages, the first including a 5,000lb (2,268kg) increase in maximum takeoff weight. The second stage was implemented in December 1993, this including a dorsal fin of carbon fibre reinforced plastics (CFRP) and wing spoilers which 'balloon' less in flight and therefore reduce profile drag.

Stage one of the PIP was flight tested in a United Airlines 747 from May 1993. The modifications were subsequently applied to new production aircraft and also made available for retrofit.

747-400IGW: Announced in December 1997 in response to a Qantas requirement, the Increased Gross Weight (IGW) 747-400 featured a maximum takeoff weight of 910,825lb (413,150kg), strengthened wing/fuselage joint, centre body structure, and undercarriage plus additional fuel forward of the wing box to bring total capacity up to 63,403 USgal (240,005 l).

With a typical load of 420 passengers in three classes, this allowed a range of up to 7,700nm (14,262km) but the project was not proceeded with. It reappeared in April 2000 with the unofficial designation 747-400ER when it was formally proposed to several carriers in the Asia-Pacific region, notably Qantas, Cathay Pacific and Singapore Airlines.

For Boeing, offering the 747-400ER was part of the process of developing new versions of the 747 to meet future needs and to compete with the planned 550-650 seat 'double decker' Airbus A3XX. The various proposed '747X' future models and developments are discussed in a later chapter.

The 1000th 747, a 747-412 destined for Singapore Airlines is rolled out in September 1993. It was delivered the following month as 9V-SMU.

BOEING 747-400

Powerplants: Four 57,100lb (254.0kN) Pratt & Whitney PW4056; 60,200lb (267.8kN) PW4060; 62,900lb (279.8kN) PW4062; 56,500lb (251.3kN) General Electric CF6-80C2B1F; 60,200lb (267.8kN) CF6-80C2B1F1; 62,100lb (276.2kN) CF6-80C2B7F; 58,000lb (258.0kN) Rolls-Royce RB211-524G; 60,600lb (269.5kN) RB211-524H or 59,000-60,000lb (262.4-266.9kN) RB211-524G/H-T turbofans. Max fuel capacity 57,285 USgal (216,846 l).

Dimensions: Wing span 211ft 5in (64.44m); length 231ft 10in (70.66m); height 63ft 8in (19.41m); wing area 5,600sq ft (520.2m²).

Weights: 400 - operating empty 401,800-405,100lb (182,256-183,753kg); max takeoff 800,000lb (362,880kg), 833,000lb (377,849kg), 850,000lb (385,560kg) or 875,000lb (396,900kg); max zero fuel 535,000lb (242,676kg); max landing 574,000lb (260,366kg); max payload 129,900-133,200lb (58,922-60,420kg).

Accommodation: 400 - typically 420 passengers in three classes. 400D - typically 568 passengers in two classes. 400M Combi - typically six or seven pallets and 266 passengers in three classes. 400F - 30 pallets on the main deck and 32 LD1 containers in the lower hold; max payload 273,350lb (124,000kg).

Performance: 400 - max cruise 507kt (939km/h); typical cruise 488kt (904km/h); range with 420 passengers 5,930-7,270nm (10,984-13,466km) depending on powerplant and maximum weight option. 400F - range with 244,000lb (110,678kg) payload 4,300nm (7,965km)

Military 747s

A relatively small proportion of 747 production has been for military or government use, although some specialist versions have been produced for the US Air Force. The following summarises those, planned versions and others which have been supplied to foreign air forces.

E-4A/B: The USAF announced selection of the 747-200 as the basis of its E-4 Advanced Airborne National Command Post (AABNCP) programme in February 1973. Alternatively known as the National Emergency Airborne Command Post (NEACP or 'Kneecap'), the E-4 has also been nicknamed the 'Doomsday Plane' as it is intended to provide an airborne base from which the US President or Vice-President along with senior government and military officials can operate during a time of war - especially a nuclear conflict.

Three E-4As (USAF serial numbers 73-1676/1677 and 74-0787) were delivered in July 1973, October 1973 and October 1974 with an interim avionics fit from the Boeing EC-135 and in the case of the first two, Pratt & Whitney JT9D-7W engines. The third aircraft had the definitive General Electric CF6-50Es (military designation F103-GE-100) and the earlier aircraft were re-engined with these in 1976.

A fourth aircraft (75-0125) was delivered in August 1975 as the E-4B with substantially upgraded avionics and communications equipment. The three original aircraft were modified to E-4B standards in 1983-85.

747 ATCA: Boeing missed a significant order for the 747 by failing to win the USAF's Advanced Tanker Cargo Aircraft (ATCA) competition. The company proposed a tanker version of the 747-200F to win the contract against the McDonnell Douglas DC-10 Srs.30CF. The prototype 747 was modified to perform 'dry' aerial refuelling tests with a number of aircraft in 1972 but the competition was won by the DC-10. As the KC-10A Extender, 60 were built for the USAF.

C-19A: Designation applied to 19 Pan American 747s modified in 1985-90 with a large cargo door, strengthened main deck floor and freight handling system. The aircraft were modified for service with the USAF Civil Reserve Air Fleet (CRAF) in times of emergency, when they would supplement the regular USAF transport force by providing bulk and oversize cargo airlift capability.

VC-25A: Two 747-2G4Bs were ordered in July 1986 under the designation VC-25A to serve as presidential transports. First flown in May and October 1987 and allocated the contrived serial numbers 82-8000 and 92-9000, they were delivered to the USAF in August and December 1990.

Delivery was delayed due to difficulties in re-wiring the aircraft, necessary because of the extremely comprehensive level of communications equipment installed. The VC-25A has 239 miles (385km) of wiring, twice that of a standard 747-200B. The aircraft also have aerial refuelling capability.

The VC-25A is a 'flying White House' and like any other aircraft uses the callsign 'Air Force One' when the US President is aboard. It has a stateroom,

The prototype 747 was modified to perform 'dry' aerial refuelling tests in 1972 as part of Boeing's attempt to win the Advanced Tanker Cargo Aircraft (ATCA) contract. It is seen here hooked up to a B-52G during the trials, but the order went to McDonnell Douglas.

conference room, communications stations and accommodation for senior staff members, representatives of the press and flight and cabin crews. Up to 70 passengers and 23 crew can be carried.

The VC-25A's lower lobe is modified to incorporate self contained airstairs leading to interior stairways joining the main deck. The underfloor area is also used for general and special storage, the latter including sufficient food for up to 2000 meals.

AL-1A: An anti ballistic and cruise missile aircraft based on the 747-400F, the AL-1A is designed to acquire and track tactical theatre ballistic missiles in their boost phase and destroy them with an airborne laser mounted in a nose turret. The AL-1A will patrol at above 40,000ft (12,190m), designate a target 42 seconds after launch and destroy it with the laser 10-30 seconds after that.

(Below) Four E-4 airborne command post 747s were delivered between 1973 and 1975. This is the second of them (73-1677) which began life as an E-4A and was later converted to an E-4B with upgraded communications equipment.

(Opposite) The first of two 747 Shuttle Carrier Aircraft (the former American Airlines 747-123 N9668) with the orbiter *Enterprise* aboard. It was delivered to NASA in 1974 and was joined by a second aircraft (ex JAL) in 1988.

The Airborne Laser Programme (ABL) team comprises Boeing, TRW Space & Electronics and Lockheed Martin. The project got underway in August 1993 when proposals to the US military were made with initial contracts awarded in November 1996.

The first AL-1A was ordered in January 1998 (Boeing designation 747-4G4F) and delivered in unmodified form in January 2000 carrying the first USAF serial number of the new century (00-0001). It was the 1238th 747 off the line. The laser system was scheduled to be fitted in 2002 and up to seven AL-1As could be in operational USAF service by 2008.

Imperial Iranian Air Force: The IIAF decided to buy 747s for mainly freighting duties in 1974, initially from the second hand market. Eight ex TWA and two ex Continental Airlines 747-100s were delivered during 1975 and modified to incorporate cargo doors and other equipment. Some were subsequently modified to tanker/transports. To supplement its fleet, Iran also took delivery of four new 747-200Fs in 1977-78. Seven of the aircraft remained in service by 2000.

Japan Air Self Defence Force: The JASDF took delivery of two 747-400s in September and November 1991 for VIP and strategic transport duties.

747 Shuttle Carrier Aircraft: NASA purchased two second hand 747-100s to transport the space shuttle orbiter in piggy-back fashion to its launch site at Cape Canaveral. The 747s were also to be used for air launches so as to permit preliminary flight tests and landings to be conducted by the orbiter.

The Shuttle Carrier Aircraft (SCA) were extensively modified to incorporate the necessary mounting pylons (to carry the orbiter and separately, its external fuel tanks), the aircraft's skin was reinforced and additional bulkheads installed, and endplate fins were attached to the horizontal tail surfaces to provide directional stability when the orbiter is in place.

VC-25A 82-8000, the first of two 747 Presidential transports which were delivered in 1990. Note the lower fuselage airstairs.

The first (an ex American Airlines 747-123) was delivered to NASA in July 1974 and the first flight with the orbiter attached was in February 1977. The first separation was achieved in August 1977, the orbiter *Enterprise* released by explosive bolts to make a successful unpowered flight to a landing at Edwards Air Force Base in California.

NASA acquired a second 747 SCA in December 1988, this one a former JAL -100SR. After modification it entered service in December 1990.

Meeting Future Needs

A computer generated image of the stretched 747-600X (bottom) and -500X (centre) as proposed in 1996. A 747-400 is also shown for comparison. Had it been built, the 747-600X would have been capable of carrying 548 passengers in three classes.

In early 2000, Alitalia announced an order for five standard 747-400s In the normal course of events this would not attract too much attention in the aviation world, but this time there was some significance involved because it was the first order placed for purely passenger carrying 747s in more than a year.

Sales of the passenger 747 had slowed during the last two or three years of the 1990s and by 2000 its market was under threat from several sources - the lower capacity but longer ranging Airbus A340, the forthcoming 550-650 seat Airbus A3XX 'double decker' and the new generation of large capacity widebody twins represented by the Airbus A330 and Boeing's own 777.

The big twins have been making inroads into the market once dominated by the 747. The 777-300, for example, carries only 30-40 fewer passengers in a typical three class configuration than does a 747-400 and although it has less range is suitable for many routes. The gap narrowed in early 2000 with the launch of the 777-300LR with range to match the 747-400.

With ever more generous extended twin engined operations (ETOPS) rules, the twins are becoming more attractive on routes traditionally served by the 747. By early 2000, the North Atlantic routes were becoming dominated by the big twins which were used on more than three-quarters of the services flown by US airlines. If European operators are factored in this drops to 55 per cent but the number is steadily growing. Even this lower proportion would have been unheard of a decade earlier.

By mid 2000, some analysts were predicting that Boeing was close to launching new 747 variants offering greater range and/or seating capacity. This follows several years of speculation as to what form the '747X' will take, with several different concepts put forward over that time:

747/II: Boeing was talking about a 747 stretch as early as the mid 1970s, its 747/II studies revolving around an aircraft 50 feet (15.24m) longer than the standard aircraft and accommodating between 520 and 700 passengers. The 747/III and 747/IV with a new supercritical wing and even greater fuselage stretches were also investigated at the time but the unavailability of engines in the required 60,000lb (266.9kN) thrust class meant they remained projects only.

747-500X/600X: Two models which came close to being launched in 1996 with a planned entry to service in early 2000. Both would have had a larger, new technology wing spanning 251 feet (76.5m) and new generation Rolls-Royce Trent or GE/P&W JV1 engines. The -500X was to be stretched by 18 feet (5.5m) to an overall length of 250 feet (76.2m) and be capable of carrying 462 passengers in three classes over a range of 8,700nm (16,115km). Maximum takeoff weight was to be 1,166,000lb (528,900kg).

The 747-600X swapped range for additional payload. With gross weight of 1,186,000lb (537,970kg) and a fuselage length of 279 feet (85.0m), it would have been able to carry 548 passengers in three classes over a distance of 7,750nm (14,355km) or about 500nm (925km) further than the longest ranging 747-400.

The 747-500/600X projects foundered because Boeing could not attract enough interest from airlines to justify the $US7 billion development costs. The resulting purchase price was simply too much for the airlines.

The 747X Models

Since the demise of the 747-500/600X projects, there have been several ideas for new generation 747s under the general designations '747-400X' and '747X'. These started in 1997 with the 747-400IGW (increased gross weight) requested by Qantas (see 747-400 chapter) and re-emerged in early 2000 as the 747ER.

A stretched version for about 490 passengers in three classes was discussed in 1998, this also featuring a new wing of increased span achieved by a wing root insert which provided space for an extra 15,000 USgal (56,800 l) of fuel, a substantial 26 per cent increase over the 747-400. A longer range derivative called the -400Y with the new wing but retaining the standard fuselage length was also proposed.

Lukewarm airline interest resulted in further variations in 1999 based around combinations of the stretched -400X and the standard wing, albeit incorporating some structural and aerodynamic modifications.

A revamped version of the previous image was released in 2000 to illustrate (from top to bottom) the proposed 747-400X, 747X and 747X Stretch. By July 2000 Boeing was saying the launch of these new models was still "six to nine months" away.

Boeing meanwhile kept insisting that the market for very large airliners was not significant while Airbus held the opposite view, both manufacturers trying to talk up the market segments for which they had (or were trying to launch) a product and talk down the opposition's strengths.

By early 2000, the basic 747-400X being discussed was slightly longer (by 5ft 7in/1.72m) than the standard -400, featured the big wing and could carry 446 passenger over a range of 8,800nm (16,300km). The stretched version would have a length of around 264 feet (80.5m), accommodate 500 passengers in three classes and have a range of 7,720nm (14,300km). Maximum takeoff weight for both was 1,043,870lb (473,500kg) and an upgraded, 777 style cockpit would be incorporated.

Driven by increasing airline interest in the A3XX (which was given a marketing 'launch' in June 2000), these concepts were further refined during the first half of the year but remained basically similar under the designations 747X and 747X Stretch. At the same time, the 747-400X designation was being applied to a -400 variant retaining the original's fuselage length and wing in combination increased weights - in other words very close to the 747-400IGW or ER as mentioned above.

Boeing also began studying a stretched version of the 747-400F in early 2000 to meet anticipated air cargo needs over the next two decades. According to its surveys, world air freight traffic will triple by 2018 and the freighter fleet double to more than 1,500 units. The stretched freighter would accommodate 36 standard 96in x 125in (2.44m x 3.17m) pallets on the main deck compared to 30 in the 747-400F.

By late July 2000, Boeing had still not formally launched the 747X models but had held a 'Future Developments Symposium' for prospective customers the previous month. At that stage the company was saying that launch was "six to nine months" away (meaning the first quarter of 2001) and that the stretched versions would take about three years to develop at a cost of between $US4bn and $US6bn.

When launched, all the new 747 models will feature an upgraded 777 style flight deck with liquid crystal flat panel primary flight displays, upgraded flight management computers, a new vertical separation display, new multifunction displays and improved datalink messaging capability.

Leading data for the planned new models as of July 2000 were as follows:

747-400X: Same overall dimensions as the existing 747-400 but with the stronger -400F wing; power by four Pratt & Whitney PW4062, Rolls-Royce RB211-524H6-T-9 or General Electric CF6-80C2B5F turbofans in the 59,500-63,300lb (264.6-281.5kN) thrust class; 416 passengers in three classes or 568 in domestic high density layout; maximum takeoff weight 910,000lb (200,617kg); maximum fuel capacity 63,545 USgal (240,543 l); design range 7690nm (12,245km).

747X: Combines a slightly stretched version of the 747-400's fuselage (to 241ft 1in/73.48m) with a new, more efficient and larger wing of 17 per cent greater area and spanning 228ft 11in (69.77m); Engine Alliance (GE/P&W) or Rolls-Royce engines in the 68,000lb (302.5kN) thrust class; increased fuel capacity of 72,573 USgal (274,717 l); maximum takeoff weight increased to 1,043,000lb (473,105kg); 430-442 passengers in three classes; design range 8975nm (16,624km).

747-400X Stretch: Combines the 747X's new wing, powerplants, fuel capacity and maximum takeoff weight with a fuselage stretched by 32ft 5in (9.90) compared to the 747-400 to an overall length of 264ft 3in (80.54m); 504-522 passengers in three classes or 660 in domestic high density layout; design range 7800nm (14,448km); freighter version will have 30 per cent more cabin volume than the 747-400 and be able to carry a payload of more than 336,000lb (152,400kg).

Summary of Orders

Notes: The table summarises the 747 orders (including military) booked up to May 2000, noting the operator, model, number, engine type fitted, announcement date of first order and date of first delivery. It does not cover resales or conversions. A dash (-) in the delivery column indicates the first delivery had not been made at the time of writing.

Customer	Model	Qty	Engines	1st Order	1st Deliv
Abu Dhabi Govt	SP	1	RB211	Sept 1989	Dec 1989
Aer Lingus	100	2	JT9D	Jan 1967	Dec 1970
Aerolineas Argentinas	200B	7	JT9D	Mar 1975	Dec 1976
Air Afrique	200B	1	JT9D	April 1979	Oct 1980
Air Canada	100	5	JT9D	Feb 1968	Feb 1971
	400	3	PW4056	Jan 1989	June 1991
Air China	200M	1	JT9D	May 1986	Mar 1987
	200F	1	JT9D	May 1990	Oct 1990
	400M	8	PW4056	May 1986	Oct 1989
	400	6	PW4056	May 1990	Mar 1992
Air France	100	16	JT9D	Sept 1966	Mar 1970
	200F	9	CF6	Oct 1973	Oct 1974
	200M	11	CF6	Aug 1976	April 1977
	200B	2	CF6	April 1979	May 1979
	400	7	CF6-80	Dec 1987	Feb 1991
	400M	5	CF6-80	Dec 1987	Sept 1991
Air Gabon	200M	1	CF6	April 1977	Oct 1978
Air India	200B	11	JT9D	Mar 1967	Mar 1971
	300M	2	CF6	Aug 1987	Oct 1988
	400	6	PW4056	Aug 1991	Aug 1993
Air Madagascar	200M	1	JT9D	June 1977	Jan 1979
Air Namibia	400M	1	CF6-80	April 1999	Oct 1999
Air New Zealand	200B	5	RB211	June 1980	May 1981
	400	4	RB211-524	July 1984	Dec 1989
Air Portugal	200B	4	JT9D	Sept 1970	Feb 1972
Alitalia	100	2	JT9D	Dec 1966	May 1970
	200B	9	CF6	Dec 1966	Mar 1971
	200F	1	CF6	Sept 1979	Dec 1981
	200M	5	CF6	Sept 1979	Nov 1980
	400	5	CF6-80	Mar 2000	early 2001

Alitalia 747-243B I-DEMV, c/n 23301, line number 618.

Customer	Model	Qty	Engines	1st Order	1st Deliv
All Nippon Airways	100SR	17	CF6	Sept 1977	Dec 1978
	200B	5	CF6	Dec 1985	June 1986
	400	11	CF6-80	Oct 1986	Aug 1990
	400D	11	CF6-80	Jan 1986	Jan 1992
American Airlines	100	16	JT9D	Nov 1966	June 1970
Amiri Flight	400	1	CF6-80	Nov 1999	Nov 1999
Asiana Airlines	400	2	CF6-80	June 1989	June 1993
	400M	6	CF6-80	June 1989	Nov 1991
	400F	6	CF6-80	Sept 1990	Nov 1994
Atlas Air	400F	12	CF6-80	June 1997	July 1998
Avianca	200M	1	JT9D	Dec 1977	June 1979
Braniff Airlines	100	1	JT9D	Jan 1968	Jan 1971
	SP	3	JT9D	May 1978	Oct 1979
	200B	1	JT9D	Jan 1978	May 1979
British Airways	100	18	JT9D	Aug 1966	April 1970
	200F	1	RB211	April 1979	Sept 1980
	200M	3	RB211	Feb 1986	Feb 1987
	400	57	RB211-524	Aug 1986	June 1989
CAAC	SP	4	JT9D	Dec 1978	Feb 1980
	200M	2	JT9D	Dec 1982	Dec 1983
Cameroon Airlines	200M	1	JT9D	July 1979	Feb 1981
Canadian Airlines	400	4	CF6-80	July 1988	Dec 1990
Canadian Pacific	200B	4	JT9D	Nov 1972	Nov 1973
Cargolux	200F	2	JT9D	Dec 1977	Jan 1979
	400F	5	CF6-80	Dec 1990	Nov 1993
	400F	7	RB211-524	Oct 1997	Dec 1998
Cathay Pacific	200B	8	RB211	Feb 1978	July 1979
	200F	2	RB211	Sept 1986	Sept 1987
	300	6	RB211	April 1984	June 1985
	400	17	RB211-524	June 1986	June 1989
	400F	5	RB211-524	Feb 1990	June 1994
China Airlines	SP	4	JT9D	Feb 1976	April 1977
	200B	3	JT9D	Dec 1978	July 1979
	200M	1	JT9D	Feb 1977	April 1978
	200F	2	JT9D	Jan 1979	July 1980
	400	13	PW4056	July 1987	Feb 1990
	400F	13	PW4056	Aug 1999	-
Condor	200B	2	JT9D	April 1970	April 1971
Continental Airlines	100	4	JT9D	Oct 1966	May 1970
Delta Air Lines	100	5	JT9D	June 1967	Sept 1970

TWA 747-131 N93108, c/n 19674, line number 38.

Customer	Model	Qty	Engines	1st Order	1st Deliv
Eastern Air Lines	100	4	JT9D	June 1967	Oct 1970
Egyptair	300M	2	JT9D	June 1987	June 1988
El Al Israel Airlines	200B	4	JT9D	Jan 1968	May 1971
	200C	2	JT9D	Mar 1975	Dec 1975
	200F	1	JT9D	Jan 1979	Mar 1979
	400	4	PW4056	Dec 1990	April 1994
Eva Air	400	7	CF6-80	Oct 1989	Nov 1992
	400M	8	CF6-80	Oct 1989	Sept 1993
	400F	3	CF6-80	May 1999	-
Flying Tiger Line	200F	6	JT9D	Aug 1978	Oct 1979
Garuda Indonesia	200B	6	JT9D	Mar 1979	July 1980
	400	2	CF6-80	Nov 1990	Jan 1994
GE Capital	400	1	CF6-80	Dec 1995	June 1999
	400F	5	CF6-80	Dec 1999	-
Iberia Airlines	100	2	JT9D	April 1968	Oct 1970
	200B	6	JT9D	April 1968	Jan 1972
	200M	1	JT9D	April 1987	April 1988
ILFC	300	3	CF6	June 1987	April 1988
	400	9	CF6-80	May 1988	May 1991
	400	2	RB211–524	May 1988	Sept 1991
	400F	1	CF6-80	Jan 1999	April 1999
Iran Air	100B	1	JT9D	June 1978	Aug 1979
	SP	4	JT9D	Oct 1973	Mar 1976
	200M	2	JT9D	April 1975	Oct 1976
Iranian Air Force	200F	4	JT9D	June 1977	Dec 1977
Iraqi Airways	SP	1	JT9D	Aug 1982	Aug 1982
	200C	3	JT9D	Jan 1975	June 1976
Japan Air Lines	100	8	JT9D	June 1966	April 1970
	100SR	12	JT9D	Oct 1972	Sept 1973
	200B	24	JT9D	May 1967	Feb 1971
	200F	7	JT9D	Mar 1974	Sept 1974
	300	9	JT9D	Mar 1983	Nov 1983
	300SR	4	JT9D	Feb 1987	Dec 1987
	400	39	CF6-80	Sept 1987	Jan 1990
	400D	8	CF6-80	June 1988	Oct 1991
Japan Asia Airways	300	1	JT9D	Aug 1987	Oct 1988
Japanese Govt	400	2	CF6-80	Dec 1987	Sept 1991

JASDF 747-47C 20-1101, c/n 24730, line number 816.

Japan Airlines 747-446
JA8081, c/n 25064, line
number 851.

Customer	Model	Qty	Engines	1st Order	1st Deliv
KLM	200B	10	JT9D	Mar 1967	Jan 1971
	200M	7	CF6	July 1974	Oct 1975
	300M	3	CF6	Jan 1982	Sept 1983
	400	5	CF6-80	April 1986	May 1989
	400M	19	CF6-80	April 1986	Sept 1989
Korean Air Lines	SP	2	JT9D	April 1979	Jan 1981
	200B	6	JT9D	June 1970	May 1973
	200F	5	JT9D	April 1979	June 1980
	300	2	JT9D	April 1979	Dec 1984
	300M	1	JT9D	April 1988	Aug 1988
	400	28	PW4056	Aug 1986	June 1989
	400M	1	PW4056	April 1988	June 1990
	400F	6	PW4056	June 1990	Sept 1996
Kuwait Airways	200M	4	JT9D	June 1977	July 1978
	400M	1	CF6-80	April 1992	Nov 1994
Lufthansa	100	3	JT9D	June 1966	Mar 1970
	200B	7	JT9D	Mar 1969	May 1971
	200F	6	JT9D	Mar 1969	Mar 1972
	200M	14	CF6	May 1975	Nov 1976
	400	24	CF6-80	May 1986	May 1989
	400M	7	CF6-80	May 1986	Sept 1989
Malaysia Airlines	300M	1	JT9D	Mar 1986	July 1986
	400	2	CF6-80	Oct 1988	Sept 1990
	400	19	PW4056	Jan 1989	Aug 1992
	400M	2	CF6-80	Oct 1987	Oct 1989
Mandarin Airlines	400	1	PW4056	Sept 1994	June 1995
Martinair Holland	200C	2	CF6	Oct 1985	Feb 1987
Middle East Airlines	200M	3	JT9D	June 1974	May 1975
National	100	2	JT9D	Feb 1967	Sept 1970
Nippon Cargo	200F	6	CF6	Nov 1983	Dec 1984
Northwest Airlines	100	10	JT9D	Nov 1966	April 1970
	200B	19	JT9D	Mar 1969	Mar 1971
	200F	8	JT9D	Oct 1974	July 1975
	400	14	PW4056	Oct 1985	Jan 1989
Olympic Airways	200B	2	JT9D	March 1973	June 1973
Pakistan International	200M	2	CF6	May 1978	July 1979

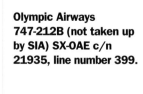

Olympic Airways
747-212B (not taken up
by SIA) SX-OAE c/n
21935, line number 399.

Customer	Model	Qty	Engines	1st Order	1st Deliv
Pan American	100	33	JT9D	April 1966	Dec 1969
	SP	10	JT9D	Sept 1973	Mar 1976
	200F	2	JT9D	June 1978	July 1979
Philippine Airlines	200B	4	CF6	Aug 1978	Dec 1979
	400	7	CF6-80	Oct 1992	Nov 1993
	400M	1	CF6-80	Jan 1996	Mar 1996
Qantas	200B	17	JT9D	Nov 1967	July 1971
	200B	5	RB211	Feb 1979	Nov 1979
	SP	2	RB211	Jan 1980	Jan 1981
	300	6	RB211	Sept 1983	Nov 1984
	400	21	RB211-524	Mar 1987	Aug 1989
Royal Air Maroc	200M	1	JT9D	May 1977	Sept 1978
Royal Jordanian	200M	2	CF6	April 1977	April 1977
	200B	1	CF6	Dec 1979	Mar 1981
Sabena	100	2	JT9D	Jan 1969	Nov 1970
	300M	2	CF6	April 1985	June 1986
SAS	200B	3	JT9D	Dec 1967	Feb 1971
	200M	3	JT9D	Sept 1976	Oct 1977
Saudi Government	SP	1	RB211	Nov 1977	July 1979
	300	1	JT9D	Dec 1983	Dec 1983
Saudia	100B	9	RB211	Dec 1979	April 1981
	SP	2	RB211	Dec 1979	June 1981
	200F	1	RB211	Dec 1988	Jan 1989
	300	10	RB211	Aug 1984	July 1985
	400	5	CF6-80	June 1995	Dec 1997
Seaboard World	200F	4	JT9D	Feb 1973	July 1974
Singapore Airlines	200B	19	JT9D	July 1972	July 1973
	200F	1	JT9D	Aug 1987	Aug 1988
	300	11	JT9D	Dec 1981	April 1983
	300M	3	JT9D	May 1983	Mar 1986
	400	43	PW4056	Mar 1986	Mar 1989
	400F	10	PW4056	Jan 1990	Aug 1994
South African Airways	200B	5	JT9D	Mar 1968	Oct 1971
	200M	2	JT9D	June 1980	Nov 1980
	SP	6	JT9D	July 1974	Mar 1976
	300	2	JT9D	June 1981	April 1983
	400	6	RB211-524	May 1989	Jan 1991
	400	2	CF6-80	Dec 1998	Dec 1998
Swissair	200B	2	JT9D	Dec 1967	Jan 1971
	300	2	JT9D	June 1980	Nov 1983
	300M	3	JT9D	Sept 1979	Mar 1983
Syrianair	SP	2	JT9D	Dec 1974	Mar 1976
Thai International	200B	6	CF6	Aug 1978	Nov 1979
	300	2	CF6	Oct 1985	Dec 1987
	400	14	CF6-80	June 1987	Feb 1990

South African Airways 747-244B ZS-SAM, c/n 20238, line number 158.

Customer	Model	Qty	Engines	1st Order	1st Deliv
Transamerica	200C	3	CF6	Oct 1978	Dec 1979
TWA	100	15	JT9D	Sept 1966	Dec 1969
	SP	3	JT9D	Oct 1978	Mar 1980
US Air Force	VC-25A	2	CF6	July 1986	Aug 1990
	E-4A	3	CF6	Feb 1973	July 1973
	E-4B	1	CF6	Dec 1973	Aug 1975
	AL-1A	1	CF6-80	Jan 1998	Jan 2000
Unidentified	400	1	CF6-80	Dec 1999	-
United Airlines	100	18	JT9D	Nov 1966	June 1970
	200B	2	JT9D	Nov 1985	Mar 1987
	400	44	PW4056	Nov 1985	June 1989
UTA	200F	3	CF6	April 1978	Sept 1978
	200M	2	CF6	June 1980	April 1981
	300	1	CF6	Aug 1981	Mar 1983
	300M	2	CF6	Aug 1981	Jan 1986
	400	1	CF6-80	July 1986	Sept 1989
	400M	1	CF6-80	July 1986	July 1991
Varig	200M	3	CF6	Jan 1981	Jan 1981
	300M	2	CF6	Oct 1984	Dec 1985
Virgin Atlantic	400	2	CF6-80	Dec 1996	June 1997
Wardair	100	1	JT9D	Nov 1972	April 1973
	200B	2	CF6	Mar 1978	June 1978
World Airways	200C	3	JT9D	Mar 1972	April 1973

Boeing 747 Summary of Orders/Deliveries
(at May 2000)

Model	Orders	Delivs
747-100	205	205
747-200	393	393
747-SP	45	45
747-300	81	81
747-400	592	517
Totals	1316	1241

Individual models (orders): 166 747-100; 10 747-100B; 29 747-100SR; 226 747-200B; 13 747-200C; 76 747-200F; 78 747-200M; 56 747-300; 21 747-300M; 4 747-300SR; 436 747-400; 19 747-400D; 74 747-400F; 63 747-400M.

Annual Orders and Deliveries

Year	Orders	Deliv	Year	Orders	Deliv
1966	85	-	1983	21	23
1967	43	-	1984	21	15
1968	22	-	1985	32	22
1969	30	3	1986	84	34
1970	18	82	1987	66	22
1971	7	72	1988	49	22
1972	18	30	1989	56	41
1973	25	29	1990	124	62
1974	31	24	1991	32	62
1975	20	16	1992	23	56
1976	14	27	1993	2	52
1977	42	19	1994	16	36
1978	71	31	1995	36	24
1979	73	67	1996	61	24
1980	47	71	1997	36	34
1981	16	52	1998	14	46
1982	11	25	1999	35	47